TOUR OF THE FOREST BIKE RACE

TOUR
OF THE FOREST
BIKE RACE

A GUIDE TO BICYCLE RACING AND THE TOUR DE FRANCE

H. E. THOMSON

Bicycle Books – San Francisco

Published by:
Bicycle Books, Inc.
P.O. Box 2038
Mill Valley, CA 94941
Tel.: (415) 381 0172
FAX: (415) 381 6912

Distributed to the book trade by:
(USA) The Talman Company, New York, NY
(UK) Chris Lloyd Sales and Marketing Services, Poole, Dorset
(Canada) Raincoast Book Distribution Ltd., Vancouver, BC

Printed in Hong Kong

Library of Congress Cataloging in Publication Data
Thomson, H. E.
Tour of the Forest Bike Race
A guide to bicycle racing and the Tour de France.
1. Bicycles and bicycling. 2. Tour de France.
I. Authorship. II. Title.

Library of Congress Catalog Card Number 90-80062

Hardcover: ISBN 933201-35-4

TO ALL MY FAMILY AND FRIENDS. SPECIAL THANKS TO THE PRICE FAMILY CIRCLE [THANKS BO AND MAT FOR TIRES AND ADVICE], KEN AND LUANNE CERVELLI, JANET BOURCHIER, AND, OF COURSE, THE CYCLISTS IN THE TOUR.

P.S. THANKS, MOM AND DAD, FOR YOUR UNENDING SUPPORT.

THE ANIMALS OF THE FOREST

LOVED SPORTS AND SPENT MUCH OF THEIR TIME
DOING THINGS LIKE...

PLAYING
HOCKEY

DOWNHILL
SKIING

TENNIS

BUT THEIR FAVORITE
SPORT OF ALL WAS
CYCLING

SWIMMING

OF COURSE, THE ANIMALS SOON BECAME
CURIOUS AS TO WHO WAS THE BETTER
CYCLIST, AND SO THEY BEGAN TO HOLD
RACES TO FIND THE FASTEST AND THE
BEST CYCLIST.

SO EACH YEAR THE ANIMALS HELD MANY RACES

SOME RACES WERE ON THE BUMPY COBBLESTONE
ROADS OF THE NORTHERN FOREST...

OTHER RACES INCLUDED STEEP AND DANGEROUS MOUNTAIN PASSES.

THEY BUILT MANY VELODROMES FOR ALL SORTS
OF TRACK RACES [THIS IS A MATCH SPRINT].

THEY HELD CRITERIUMS, WHERE THE RACERS DO
MANY LAPS AROUND A SHORT COURSE, LIKE
AROUND A BEAVERDAM.

BUT THE BIGGEST AND MOST IMPORTANT RACE WAS
THE TOUR OF THE FOREST, HELD EVERY JULY. THE TOUR
LASTED ABOUT THREE WEEKS, TAKING THE RACERS
THROUGH MOST OF THE FOREST. EACH DAY THERE WAS A

RACE [CALLED A STAGE], AND WHOEVER HAD THE
BEST COMBINED TIME AFTER THE LAST STAGE WON.

BECAUSE THE TOUR OF THE FOREST WAS SO
LONG AND SO TOUGH, YOU NEEDED A STRONG
TEAM TO HELP YOU WIN. MOST TEAMS HAVE :

A LEADER [THEIR
BEST CYCLIST]

A ROAD CAPTAIN [WHO
HELPS ORGANIZE THE
TEAM DURING THE RACE]

A SPRINTER
[TO WIN SPRINTS]

AND SUPPORT RIDERS WHO HELP THE TEAM
LEADER .

HERE ARE A FEW OF THE TEAMS IN THE TOUR:

THE CAT ATHLETIC SQUAD [CAS]

THE SYSTÈME-ROO TEAM

AND THE SKUNK TEAM [PHEW-GO]

JERSEYS

SINCE THE TOUR OF THE FOREST WAS SO LONG, IT HELPED TO KNOW WHO WAS IN THE LEAD EACH DAY. SO THE RIDER WITH THE BEST TIME ALWAYS WORE A BRIGHT YELLOW JERSEY SO EVERYONE COULD SAY, "HEY, HE'S IN THE LEAD."

BUT THERE WERE OTHER CATEGORIES TO WIN JERSEYS IN . . .

THERE WERE TWO JERSEYS FOR SPRINTERS TO WIN: A RED ONE FOR THE BEST SPRINTER IN THE INTERMEDIATE SPRINTS [WHICH WERE AT MARKED POINTS DURING EACH STAGE]; AND A GREEN ONE FOR THE BEST SPRINTER AT THE FINISH LINES OF THE STAGES.

THE BEST CLIMBER
GOT A NEAT RED
POLKA-DOT JERSEY

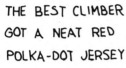

MAN I
HATE HILLS

THE BEST NEWCOMER WORE
A WHITE JERSEY

THE WILDEST JERSEY WAS THE PATCHWORK
JERSEY WHICH ,BESIDES BEING A FASHION
STATEMENT, WENT TO THE MOST CONSISTENT
CYCLIST IN ALL THESE EVENTS.

AFTER EACH STAGE, THE OFFICIALS WORKED OUT THE
TIMES AND THE MOUNTAIN AND SPRINT POINTS
OF THE RACERS.

WHOEVER WAS LEADING IN EACH CATEGORY AT THE
END OF THE STAGE GOT TO WEAR THE JERSEY FOR
THAT CATEGORY IN THE NEXT STAGE.

BECAUSE THERE WERE SO MANY STAGES IN THE TOUR,
THESE JERSEYS COULD CHANGE HANDS MANY TIMES
DURING THE RACE, AND WHOEVER WAS WEARING THE
YELLOW JERSEY AFTER THE LAST STAGE WAS THE
WINNER OF THE TOUR OF THE FOREST.

TYPES OF RACES IN THE TOUR

THE TOUR ORGANIZERS WANTED TO MAKE SURE THAT THE OVERALL WINNER WAS THE BEST CYCLIST IN THE EVENT, SO THEY ALWAYS HAD THREE DIFFERENT TYPES OF RACES IN THE TOUR:

1 TIME TRIALS

2 TEAM TIME TRIALS

3 ROAD RACES

TIME TRIALS — IN THIS KIND OF STAGE THE RACERS LEAVE THE STARTING LINE ONE AFTER ANOTHER AND TRY TO COVER THE COURSE AS FAST AS POSSIBLE BECAUSE THEY ARE RACING AGAINST THE CLOCK. THE RACERS USE "FUNNY" BIKES WITH SOLID DISK WHEELS THAT ARE MORE AERODYNAMIC.

TIME TRIALS COULD BE ANYWHERE BETWEEN 10 TO 80 KILOMETERS LONG.

TEAM TIME TRIALS - THESE ARE THE SAME AS TIME TRIALS—BUT
INSTEAD OF EACH RACER GOING BY HIMSELF,
EACH TEAM RODE THE COURSE TOGETHER.

THE TEAMS RIDE IN FORMATION AND THE TEAM
MEMBERS TAKE TURNS BREAKING THE WIND AT THE
FRONT WHILE THE OTHERS SAVE ENERGY DRAFTING
BEHIND.

HOWEVER, MOST OF THE TOUR'S TWENTY ODD STAGES WERE
ROAD RACES WHERE ALL THE CYCLISTS START AT ONCE AND

EVERYONE TRIES TO GET TO THE FINISH LINE FIRST. ROAD
RACES COULD OFTEN BE OVER 200 KILOMETERS LONG!

PEOPLE WHO HELP DURING THE RACE

MECHANICS FOLLOW THE CYCLISTS WITH SPARE WHEELS AND BIKES

OFFICIALS KEEP TIME AND MAKE SURE EVERYONE PLAYS FAIR [OFFICIALS ARE ALSO WELL-DRESSED]

REPORTERS FILM AND WRITE ABOUT THE RACE

MEDICS HELP INJURED CYCLISTS

OTHERS HELP TOO

THE DIRECTEUR-SPORTIF
[THE COACH]...

I THINK YOU SHOULD
TRY A NEW HAIRSTYLE

PLANS THE TEAM'S STRATEGY AND GIVES HIS RACERS
ADVICE DURING THE RACE.

MEATWAGON
ADVENTURE
TEAM

TEAM MECHANICS FIX AND CLEAN THE TEAM'S BIKES
AFTER EACH STAGE.

THE SOIGNEURS [THE TRAINERS] HAND BAGS OF FOOD TO THEIR TEAM'S CYCLISTS DURING THE RACE AND GIVE THEM MASSAGES AFTERWARDS.

AND SPECTATORS HELP TIRED CYCLISTS UP MOUNTAINS.

TYPES OF CYCLISTS

[MOST CYCLISTS ARE BETTER AT ONE THING]

SPRINTERS-THEY LIKE TO SAVE ENERGY IN THE PACK DURING THE RACE...

←— SPRINTER

AND THEN SPRINT AWAY IN THE LAST FEW HUNDRED METERS.

CLIMBERS- THEY ARE USUALLY SMALL ANIMALS LIKE
RABBITS AND HAMSTERS [AND OTHER
RODENT-LIKE CREATURES] WHO CAN GO
UPHILL VERY FAST.

IT'S IMPORTANT NOT TO LOOK HAPPY WHILE CLIMBING
[PHOTOGRAPHERS WON'T TAKE YOUR PICTURE IF YOU DO].
SO HERE ARE SOME ACCEPTABLE EXPRESSIONS FOR
CLIMBING...

SUCKING IN
AIR

TONGUE OUT

GRITTING
TEETH

EXHAUSTED

GENERALLY SPEAKING, SPRINTERS ARE REALLY POOR
CLIMBERS AND CLIMBERS ARE TERRIBLE SPRINTERS.

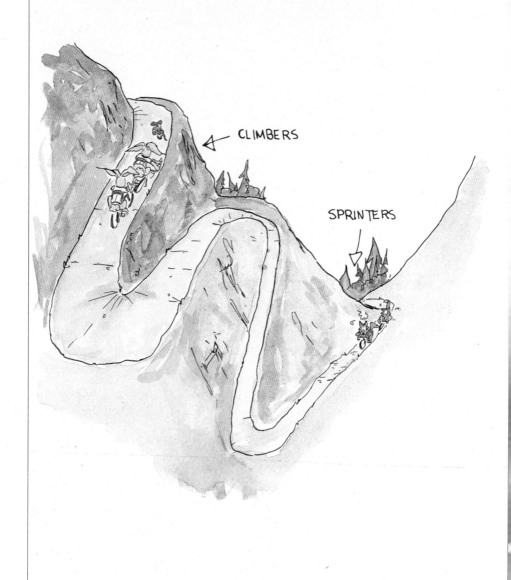

CLIMBERS

SPRINTERS

TIME TRIALISTS-THEY CAN PEDAL VERY FAST FOR LONG
PERIODS OF TIME, AND BECAUSE OF THIS
THE STRONGEST TIME TRIALISTS ARE
USUALLY AMONG THE TOP RACERS IN
THE TOUR.

TIME TRIALISTS OFTEN WIN RACES BY BREAKING AWAY
FROM THE PACK AND USING THEIR ABILITIES TO STAY
AWAY. BADGERS MAKE GOOD TIME TRIALISTS.

DOMESTIQUES - THEY ARE THE TEAM WORKERS. THESE CYCLISTS ARE NOT STRONG ENOUGH TO WIN THE TOUR - BUT THEY ARE VERY IMPORTANT TO THEIR TEAMS.

IF THE TEAM'S STAR RIDER HAS A FLAT OR WRECKS HIS BIKE, A DOMESTIQUE WILL GIVE UP A WHEEL OR HIS BIKE.

THEY DROP BACK TO THE TEAM CAR TO PICK UP FOOD AND WATER.

AND THEY WORK HARD PULLING THEIR LEADER INTO POSITION TO WIN.

WHAT CYCLISTS WEAR

[CYCLISTS DON'T WEAR NORMAL CLOTHING]

CYCLING JERSEYS HAVE THREE POCKETS IN THE BACK, SO THE RACERS CAN CARRY FOOD AND OTHER THINGS THEY MIGHT NEED IN THE RACE.

POCKETS

CYCLING SHOES HAVE REALLY STIFF SOLES AND CLEATS TO LOCK THEM INTO THE PEDALS

CLEAT

CYCLING SHORTS ARE MADE OF STRETCHY CLOTH CALLED LYCRA AND HAVE PADDING IN THE SEAT TO MAKE RIDING MORE COMFORTABLE. MANY PROFESSIONALS USE "BIB" SHORTS WITH BUILT-IN SUSPENDERS.

GLOVES HAVE LEATHER PALMS TO PROTECT YOUR HANDS IN A FALL

IN TIME TRIALS THE RACERS WEAR A SKINSUIT, WHICH
IS LIKE A LYCRA JERSEY AND SHORTS PUT TOGETHER
SO THEY ARE REALLY SLEEK.

PROFESSIONAL CYCLISTS OFTEN WEAR A COTTON HAT OR A
HEADBAND WITH THEIR TEAM'S NAME ON IT [BUT YOU
REALLY SHOULD ALWAYS WEAR A HELMET FOR PROTECTION].

AND, OF COURSE, A PAIR OF COOL SUNGLASSES TO TOP
ALL THIS OFF.

BUT BECAUSE THE RACE WENT ON NO MATTER WHAT
THE WEATHER-RAIN OR SNOW —THE RACERS NEEDED
CLOTHES FOR THE COLD.

LIKE ARM AND LEG WARMERS AND RAIN JACKETS

Hole for
CLEAT

BOOTIES AND GLOVES TO KEEP THEIR PAWS TOASTY
WARM, AND OF COURSE, NEWSPAPER.

YES, THAT IS CORRECT - NEWSPAPER.

AFTER SWEATING ALL THE WAY TO THE TOP OF A
COLD MOUNTAIN, THE RACERS NEED SOMETHING TO KEEP
THEM WARM ON THE DESCENT—SO THEY STUFF A
NEWSPAPER UP THEIR JERSEY.

BICYCLES

THE RACERS USE TWO TYPES OF BIKES IN THE TOUR:

A ROAD BIKE FOR ROAD RACES

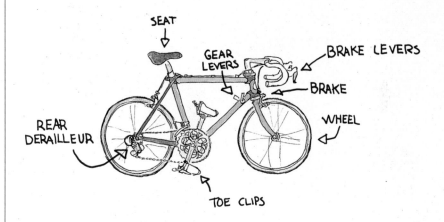

SEAT

GEAR LEVERS

BRAKE LEVERS

BRAKE

WHEEL

REAR DERAILLEUR

TOE CLIPS

A FUNNY BIKE FOR TIME TRIALS

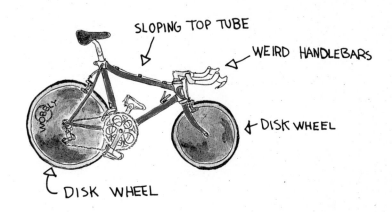

SLOPING TOP TUBE

WEIRD HANDLEBARS

DISK WHEEL

WOBBLY

DISK WHEEL

ANIMALS THAT DO NOT MAKE GOOD BIKE RACERS

ELEPHANTS ARE TOO HEAVY AND IT IS VERY HARD TO FIND JERSEYS THAT FIT THEM

MOOSE MAKE BETTER BIKE RACKS

SNAKES ARE ALWAYS GETTING CAUGHT IN THE SPOKES

TURTLES DO NOT HAVE VERY FAST LEG MUSCLES

FISH DO NOT HAVE A KEEN GRASP OF THE CYCLING SCENE

WHALES DO NOT LIKE BEING OUT OF THE WATER AND HAVE TROUBLE PEDALLING

PORCUPINES FLAT OUT TOO MUCH

GIRAFFES HAVE POOR AERODYNAMICS

SLOTHS DO NOT HAVE ENOUGH MOTIVATION

BATS CAN'T SEE THE RACE COURSE

SOME CYCLING TERMS

BONK- WHEN YOU TOTALLY
RUN OUT OF ENERGY

WHEELSUCKER- SOMEONE WHO
WON'T TAKE A
TURN BREAKING
THE WIND

CYCLOCROSS- THIS IS ANOTHER TYPE OF
RACE WHERE THE CYCLISTS
CARRY THEIR BIKES OVER
OBSTACLES AND THROUGH
MUD

MUD

TRACKSTAND- WHEN YOU BALANCE
ON YOUR BIKE IN ONE
SPOT WITHOUT FALLING
OVER

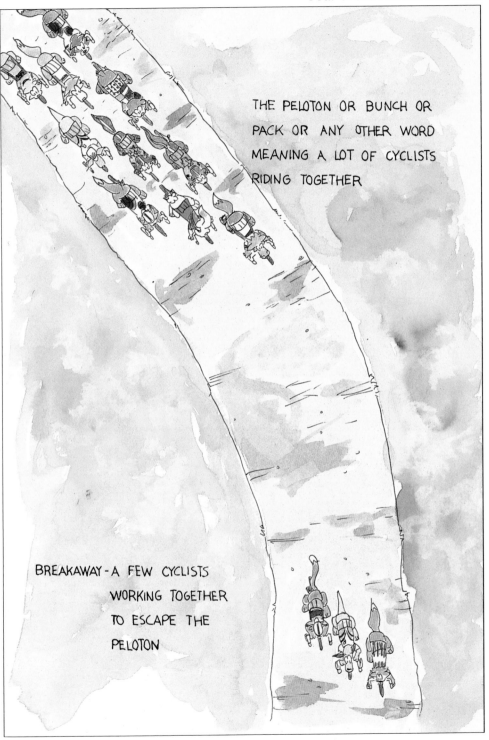

THE PELOTON OR BUNCH OR
PACK OR ANY OTHER WORD
MEANING A LOT OF CYCLISTS
RIDING TOGETHER

BREAKAWAY - A FEW CYCLISTS
WORKING TOGETHER
TO ESCAPE THE
PELOTON

A WIPE-OUT

WIPE-OUTS ARE VERY PAINFUL AND TIME CONSUMING. THEY SHOULD BE AVOIDED AS MUCH AS POSSIBLE.

BLOW UP-WHEN YOU CAN NO LONGER KEEP UP THE PACE. THIS IS ALSO VERY TIME CONSUMING.

ROAD RASH-WHAT CYCLISTS HAVE AFTER A WIPE-OUT

CHASE GROUP- A GROUP OF RIDERS IN FRONT OF THE
PELOTON TRYING TO CATCH THE BREAK

PELOTON   CHASE GROUP   BREAKAWAY

MUSETTE -THE BAG OF FOOD HANDED TO THE CYCLISTS

43

A TYPICAL TOUR

ALTHOUGH THE ROUTE OF THE TOUR OF THE FOREST
CHANGED EACH YEAR, A MAP OF A TYPICAL TOUR
WOULD LOOK SOMETHING LIKE THIS :

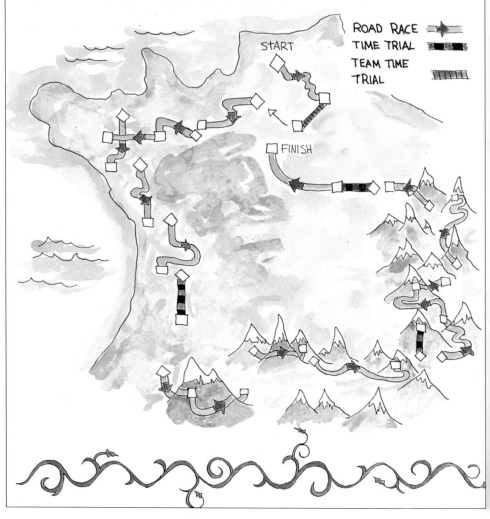

THE FIRST DAY OF THE TOUR IS ALWAYS A PROLOGUE.
THIS IS A VERY SHORT TIME TRIAL [USUALLY UNDER
TEN KILOMETERS] AND IT GIVES THE SPECTATORS A
QUICK GLIMPSE OF ALL THE RACERS.

THE PROLOGUE ALSO
GIVES THE TOUR ITS
FIRST RACE LEADER.

STAGE 1: ROAD RACE

STAGE 2: TEAM TIME TRIAL

THE TEAM LEADERS DO NOT PARTICULARLY
ENJOY THIS STAGE BECAUSE THEY GET THE
SAME TIME AS THEIR TEAM; SO IF THEY
HAVE TO WAIT FOR A SLOW TEAM MEMBER
THEY COULD LOSE TIME TO OTHER TEAMS.

STAGES 3 TO 8: ROAD RACES

> THESE ARE GENERALLY RACES ON FLATTER
> ROADS THAT FAVOUR THE SPRINTERS. ALSO,
> SINCE THERE ARE HARDER STAGES TO COME,
> THE STARS OFTEN LET A DOMESTIQUE ESCAPE
> TO WIN A STAGE IN THIS PART OF THE RACE.

STAGE 9: A LONGISH TIME TRIAL.

THIS IS A REALLY IMPORTANT STAGE BECAUSE
IN ORDER TO WIN THE TOUR, A CYCLIST ALWAYS
MUST DO WELL IN THE TIME TRIALS; AND
THIS FIRST ONE IS WHERE THE REAL CONTENDERS
START TO MOVE UP IN THE STANDINGS.

LIKE GO MAN

COACH GIVING INSTRUCTIONS

THE RACERS ARE USUALLY FOLLOWED BY SOMEBODY
TO TELL THEM HOW THEY ARE DOING AND IN
CASE THEY NEED TO CHANGE WHEELS OR BIKES.

STAGES 10 TO 14: ROAD RACES IN THE MOUNTAINS
THIS IS WHERE THE TOUR GETS REALLY HARD.

CLIMBERS TRY TO MAKE UP GROUND THEY LOST DURING
THE FLAT STAGES, AND SPRINTERS JUST TRY TO MAKE
IT UP THE MOUNTAINS.

AFTER THESE MOUNTAIN STAGES, THE RACERS GET A
DAY OFF.

BUT THEY DO NOT SPEND THE WHOLE DAY LYING AROUND;
THEY RIDE THEIR BIKES ABOUT FOUR HOURS AND INSPECT
THE COURSE FOR THE NEXT DAY.

STAGE 15: UPHILL TIME TRIAL

      THIS IS NOT A FUN STAGE

STAGES 16 TO 21 : MORE ROAD RACES IN THE MOUNTAINS

SOMETIME DURING THIS PART OF THE RACE, THE RACERS GET ANOTHER REST DAY.

CERTAIN MOUNTAINS ARE VERY IMPORTANT BECAUSE
THEY ARE SO STEEP AND HARD TO CLIMB. RACERS
THEN COULD LOSE A LOT OF TIME ON THESE CLIMBS.
ONE OF THE MOST FAMOUS MOUNTAINS IS YELP-DO-
WHEEZE WITH ITS 21 SWITCHBACKS.

STAGE 22: ONE LAST TIME TRIAL

ALTHOUGH THIS TIME TRIAL IS USUALLY NOT THAT LONG, IT IS VERY IMPORTANT; IF THE OVER-ALL STANDINGS ARE CLOSE, THIS STAGE COULD DECIDE THE WINNER.

THIS BETTER BE THE LAST ONE

IN ALL THE TIME TRIALS, THE RACERS START IN REVERSE ORDER [MEANING THE RACER IN LAST PLACE OVER-ALL WENT FIRST AND THE RACER WITH THE YELLOW JERSEY WENT LAST].

STAGE 23: THE LAST ROAD RACE
IT ENDS IN THE CAPITAL OF THE FOREST.

AFTER THE TIME TRIAL THE WINNER OF THE TOUR HAS
BEEN DECIDED AND THE YELLOW JERSEY JUST HAS
TO RIDE SAFELY INTO THE CAPITAL WITH THE PELOTON.

THE FINAL SPRINT OF THE TOUR IS DOWN THE MAIN
STREET AND OF ALL THE STAGES, THIS LAST ONE IS THE
ONE THE SPRINTERS WANT TO WIN.

AFTER THE TOUR OF THE FOREST ENDS, THEY THROW A
BIG PARTY BECAUSE EVERYONE IS SO RELIEVED THE RACE
IS OVER [ESPECIALLY THE WINNER] AND THEY DANCE
AROUND ALL NIGHT DRINKING ROOTBEER.

THE NEXT DAY EVERYONE STARTS TRAINING FOR NEXT YEAR.

THE END

Appendix:
How to Become a
Pro Bike Racer

NOW AFTER READING THIS BOOK YOU MIGHT BE ASKING
YOURSELF, "HOW CAN I BECOME A PROFESSIONAL CYCLIST?"

WELL, IT IS QUITE SIMPLE TO ENTER THIS GLAMOROUS
PROFESSION. JUST RIDE YOUR BIKE SIX HOURS EACH
AND EVERY DAY.

THEN ONE DAY YOU WILL SAY TO YOURSELF, "I HATE
BIKING!"

GADS I HATE BIKING!

YOU ARE NOW READY TO JOIN THE PRO RANKS.

Photograph by Michael Slawinski

About the Author

H. E. Thomson is a native of Rossland, British Columbia, but reluctantly resides in Alberta, where he is finishing a degree in History at the University of Calgary, and plans to continue on in the Art History program. Having the best of both worlds — being a starving student as well as a starving artist —, his main function is as a tax write-off for his parents.

Thanks to boring classes throughout his academic career, he has been able to refine his art so his characters actually resemble animals. Although his technical ability may suggest otherwise, major influences on his development have been Hiroshige, Gustav Klimt, and Richard Scarry. Along with crashing his bicycle, his main interests are pestering Bob Price's cat and building guitars.

In High Gear
The world of professional bicycle racing
Samuel Abt

*208 pages text plus 16-page photo insert
Paperback, 6 x 9 inches (152 x 228mm)
ISBN 0-933201-34-6*

*Just like the animals of the forest, adult
humans also race bicycles. This is
where you read about it all. In recent
years, more and more American and
other English-speaking athletes have
entered the fascinating world of
professional bicycle racing, long the
domain of European racers. Samuel Abt
gives the inside story on the
international racing scene and the life of
the professional bicycle racer. The book
has been updated to include full
coverage of the exciting 1989 season,
culminating in Greg LeMond's successes in both the Tour de France and the
World Championships.*

Major Taylor
The extraordinary career of a champion bicycle racer
Andrew Ritchie

*304 pages plus 32-page photo insert
Hardcover, 6 x 9 inches (152 x 228mm)
ISBN 0-933201-14-1*

*Read the fascinating story of Major
Taylor, the black American professional
bicycle racer who was the most popular
sportsman in the world. Admired and
fondly remembered to this day in France
and Australia, Taylor was largely
forgotten in the US. Ritchie's book rights
this wrong. Although the movie rights to
this book have recently been sold, we
suggest you read the book while waiting
for the movie.*

The
Bicycle Racing
Guide

Rob Van der Plas

Technique and training for bicycle racers and triathletes

The Bicycle Racing Guide

Technique and training for bicycle racers and triathletes
Rob van der Plas
256 pages with over 250 illustrations
Paperback, 6 x 9 inches (152 x 228mm)
ISBN 0-933201-13-3)
This is the most authoritative guide to training for bicycle racing. Written primarily for the amateur racer — whether male or female, whether working alone or under the guidance of a coach — this book provides all the information needed for effective training and successful racing on the road, on the track and in cyclo-cross events. Includes equipment selection and nutritional guidance, as well as detailed training schedules.

The New Bike Book

How to get the most out of your new bike
Jim Langley
128 pages with more than 50 clear and simple illustrations.

Paperback, 6 x $4^3/8$ inches (152 x 110mm)
ISBN 0-933201-28-1
This is the right book for the less ambitious bicycle rider. It does not show you how to win the Tour, but it is easy to read and packed with sound advice for the novice who just wants to enjoy riding his or her bike comfortably and efficiently.

Ordering books published by Bicycle Books, Inc.

All books published by Bicycle Books, Inc. may be obtained through the book or bike trade. If not available locally, use the coupon below to order directly from the publisher. Allow three weeks for delivery.

Fill out coupon and send to: **Bicycle Books, Inc.**
PO Box 2038
Mill Valley CA 94941 (USA)
FAX (415) 381 6912

Please include payment in full *(check or money order made out to Bicycle Books, Inc.). If not paid in advance, books will be sent UPS COD.*
Canadian and other foreign customers please note: *Prices quoted are in US Dollars. Postage and handling fee for foreign orders is $2.50 per book. Payment in US currency (enquire at your bank) must be enclosed.*

Please send the following books:

The Mountain Bike Book	_____ copies @ $10.95 =	$ _____
The Bicycle Repair Book	_____ copies @ $8.95 =	$ _____
The Bicycle Racing Guide	_____ copies @ $10.95 =	$ _____
The Bicycle Touring Manual	_____ copies @ $10.95 =	$ _____
Roadside Bicycle Repairs	_____ copies @ $4.95 =	$ _____
Major Taylor (hardcover)	_____ copies @ $19.95 =	$ _____
Bicycling Fuel	_____ copies @ $7.95 =	$ _____
Mountain Bike Maintenance	_____ copies @ $7.95 =	$ _____
In High Gear	_____ copies @ $10.95 =	$ _____
The Bicycle Fitness Book	_____ copies @ $7.95 =	$ _____
The Bicycle Commuting Book	_____ copies @ $7.95 =	$ _____
The New Bike Book	_____ copies @ $4.95 =	$ _____
Tour of the Forest Bike Race	_____ copies @ $9.95 =	$ _____
Bicycle Technology	_____ copies @ $16.95 =	$ _____

Sub total $ _____
California residents add sales tax $ _____
Shipping and handling (within US):
$2.50 first book, $1.00 each additional book $ _____

Total amount $ _____

Name _____
Address _____
City, _____
State, zip _____ Tel.: (___)_____
MC / VISA No._____ Signature _____